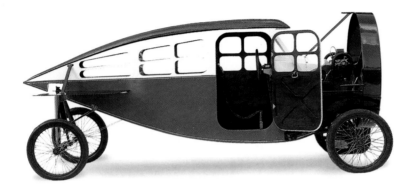

SNAP SHOT™

Senior Editor
Mary Ling

Art Editor
Joanna Pocock

Designer
Helen Melville

Production
Catherine Semark

Consultant
Miriam Farbey

US Editor
Camela Decaire

A SNAPSHOT™ BOOK

Snapshot™ is an imprint of Covent Garden Books
95 Madison Avenue
New York, NY 10016

Photography by Paul Bricknell, Andy Crawford,
Peter Downs, Mike Dunning, Dave King,
Richard Leeney, Dave Rudkin, James Stevenson,
Clive Streeter

Picture credits: Balloon Base (Bristol – UK): 24tl;
British Library: 12c; British Museum: 4tl;
National Maritime Museum: 10tr; 26tl, 27t, 27b;
Science Museum: 11c.

ISBN 1-56458-956-0

Color reproduction by Colourscan
Printed in Belgium by Proost

INCREDIBLE
INVENTIONS

Written by
Philip Wilkinson

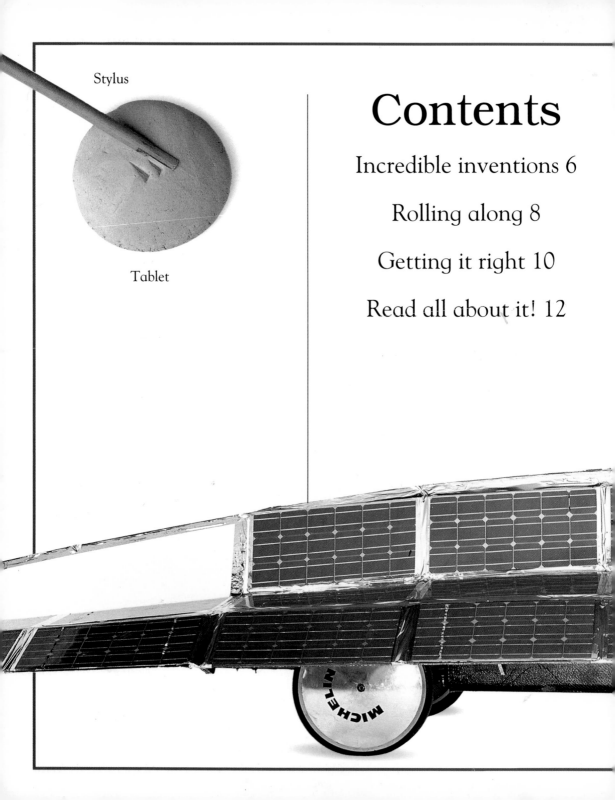

Stylus

Tablet

Contents

Solar Flair

Incredible inventions

Inventions are all around us, from the ballpoint pen to the zipper. Whatever we do, wherever we go, we rely on the ideas of inventors.

A moving ball transfers ink to paper.

Tube of quick-drying ink

An invention is a thing that didn't exist before

Keep on plowing
Plows turn soil over for planting. They were invented over 5,000 years ago in the Middle East!

Ballpoint pen with lid

No more blobs!
Hungarians Georg and Josef Biro invented a kind of ballpoint pen, the Biro.

Strike a light!
Modern matches appeared in 1827. They were coated in chemicals such as sulfur, which ignites when rubbed on sandpaper.

Matches

Zip, zip
Zippers were invented in 1893.
Look how many zippers you have
on your clothes. Can you see
how a metal slider pulls two
rows of tiny hooks together?

*Row of
metal hooks*

Slider

Zipper

Snip, snip
Scissors have been around
for about 3,000 years, and
were probably invented
independently in different
parts of the world.

Blades

Measure up
Ancient Egyptians made
standard-length metal chains to
measure distance.
Modern tape
measures
roll up.

Nut

Scissors

somebody thought of it.

*Winder pulls
tape into case.*

19th-century linen
tape measure

*Metal knife
cuts through soil.*

Plow

Rolling along

The wheel is a simple but incredibly useful object now used on road and rail vehicles everywhere.

The wheel was invented

Stephenson's Rocket

Early wheels were solid disks of wood or stone.

The Rocket was built in 1829.

Robert Stephenson, George's son, designed most of the Rocket.

Spoked wheels first appeared about 4,000 years ago.

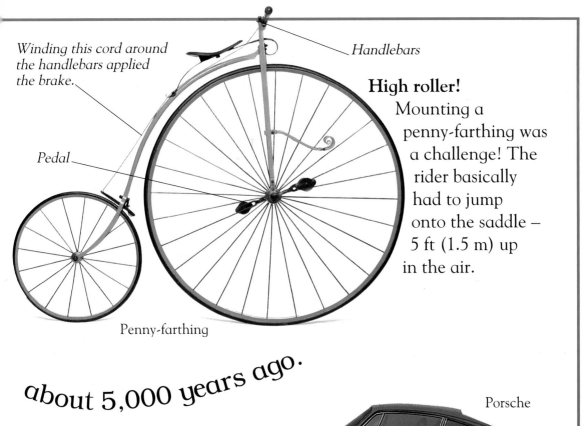

Winding this cord around the handlebars applied the brake.

Handlebars

Pedal

Penny-farthing

High roller!

Mounting a penny-farthing was a challenge! The rider basically had to jump onto the saddle – 5 ft (1.5 m) up in the air.

about 5,000 years ago.

Porsche

Steaming along

Trains use wheels to run on tracks. This steam engine, called the *Rocket,* was built by George Stephenson in 1829, and was the first vehicle that could move faster than a horse.

Hitting the road

This Porsche looks very different from the first car, built by Carl Benz in 1885. His tricycle chugged along at 8 mph (13 kph), but it used an internal combustion engine similar to the engines on modern cars.

Getting it right

When people started to travel, there were things they needed to know – like what direction to take and when they would get there!

Dragon holds bronze ball.

Which way?
Third-century Chinese navigators noticed that lodestone, a mineral containing magnetic iron, always points North-South. This was the first compass.

You always know

Did the Earth move?
The ancient Chinese invented this earthquake detector: when there's a tremor, the dragons open their mouths and drop the bronze balls into the mouths of the toads below. Today a seismograph gives accurate, advance warning.

Toad waits to catch ball.

Roman steelyard

Beam with scale

This Roman steelyard is from the ancient city of Pompeii.

Compass

Metal weight

How heavy?
To measure weight with these scales, the metal weight is moved until the beam balances. The numbers on the beam give the weight in the pan.

where you are with a compass.

What time is it?
Mechanical clocks were probably first made in the early 15th century. They were huge machines, more than 3 ft (1 m) high, but nowhere near as accurate as a modern wristwatch.

Wristwatch

Scale pan

Read all about it!

Printing began the first information revolution. Computers and CD-ROMs are beginning the next.

Gutenberg's first printed book was the Bible.

Platen presses down onto type.

On press
A German, Johannes Gutenberg, developed a movable type printing process around 1447. After one page was printed, the letters were separated and reused.

Screen

Keyboard

On screen
With modern laptop computers we can access and store information anywhere. Data can be kept on the machine's own hard drive, or come down a phone line to the computer.

Tympan is placed between type and paper.

On disc
A CD-ROM can store video, cartoons, sound, and words. Any image can be instantly displayed on a computer screen.

Metal type is placed on the stone.

Ink ball

William Caxton set up the first printing press in England in 1447.

500 million letters on one disc!

Power to the people

Animal muscles, flowing water, wind, natural gas, the Sun – all are sources of power that people have learned how to harness.

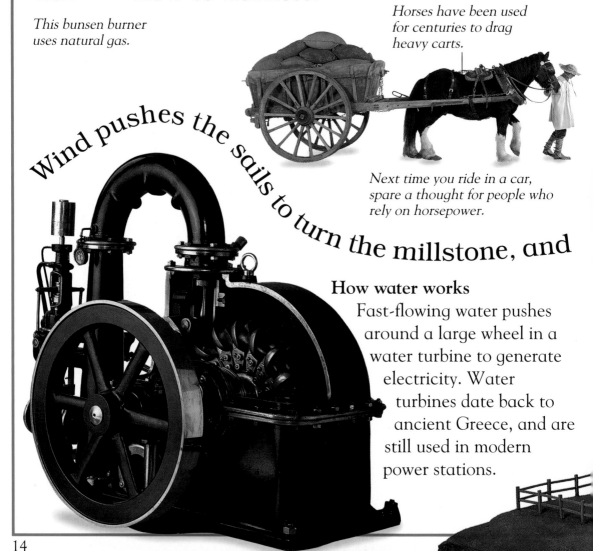

This bunsen burner uses natural gas.

Horses have been used for centuries to drag heavy carts.

Wind pushes the sails to turn the millstone, and

Next time you ride in a car, spare a thought for people who rely on horsepower.

How water works
Fast-flowing water pushes around a large wheel in a water turbine to generate electricity. Water turbines date back to ancient Greece, and are still used in modern power stations.

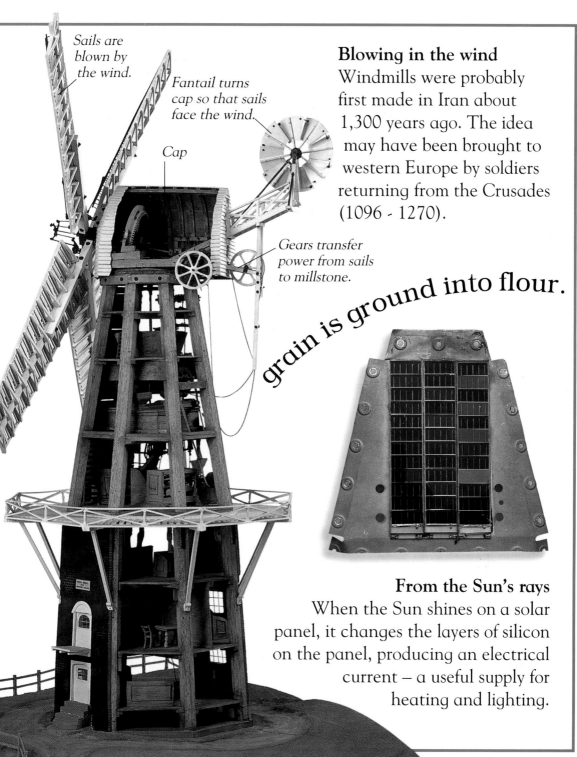

Sails are blown by the wind.

Fantail turns cap so that sails face the wind.

Cap

Gears transfer power from sails to millstone.

Blowing in the wind
Windmills were probably first made in Iran about 1,300 years ago. The idea may have been brought to western Europe by soldiers returning from the Crusades (1096 - 1270).

grain is ground into flour.

From the Sun's rays
When the Sun shines on a solar panel, it changes the layers of silicon on the panel, producing an electrical current – a useful supply for heating and lighting.

Flick of a switch

We all want warmth, light, and comfort in our homes. In the 20th century, electricity has provided the power.

Lightbulb

On air

The first radio messages were sent by Italian inventor Guglielmo Marconi in 1895. By the 1920s, regular broadcasts brought radio into the home.

1930s valve radio

Electricity is a form of energy.

1925 electric hair dryer

Getting dry

This early hair dryer was made in 1925. Inside, there is a fan and an electric heater with two heat settings. It is very like the hair dryers of today.

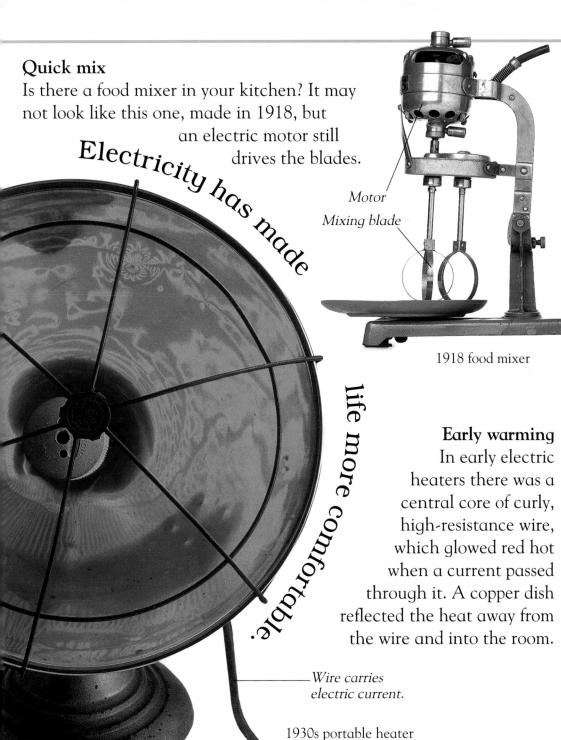

Quick mix

Is there a food mixer in your kitchen? It may not look like this one, made in 1918, but an electric motor still drives the blades.

Electricity has made

Motor

Mixing blade

1918 food mixer

life more comfortable.

Early warming

In early electric heaters there was a central core of curly, high-resistance wire, which glowed red hot when a current passed through it. A copper dish reflected the heat away from the wire and into the room.

Wire carries electric current.

1930s portable heater

It's for you!

Smoke signals, mirrors, and flags were once the only way to "talk" to somebody too far away to hear you shout. Things suddenly changed in the 1800s.

Semaphore is a signaling system using flags.

Tapping out the message

In 1844, Samuel Morse sent a message along a wire. His "Morse code" could tap out the alphabet in long and short sounds transcribed as dots and dashes.

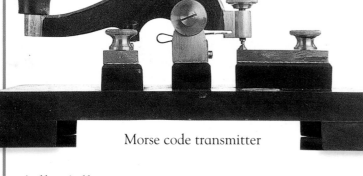

Morse code transmitter

'ello, 'ello

Alexander Graham Bell developed the telephone in 1876. When he spoke into a tube, the vibrations of his voice became electrical signals that were transmitted to a second telephone.

Mouthpiece

Box telephone

Tube

On the move

Until recently, all telephones were connected by wires. With radio and computer technology, engineers have created cordless mobile telephones that will work almost anywhere.

Mobile
telephone

The word "telephone" means "far voice."

Earpiece

1930s "cradle"
telephone

EMERGENCY CALLS
FOR
FIRE
POLICE | DIAL
AMBULANCE | 999
LARKSWOOD
4524

Think of a number
With the first telephones, every call was made via the operator. By the 1920s, telephones had direct dialing. Modern phones have push button dialing.

19

See it, hear it

Toward the end of the 19th century, sounds and moving pictures were recorded for the first time. Home entertainment was transformed.

Phenakistoscope

In a spin
A first attempt at producing a moving image was the phenakistoscope. As this phenakistoscope spins, the man eats his dinner.

Sound was first recorded in 1877 by

Polaroid camera

Instant picture
Edwin H. Land announced his instant black-and-white picture camera in 1947. The color version was created in 1963.

The picture develops before your eyes.

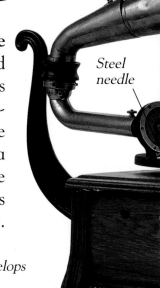

Steel needle

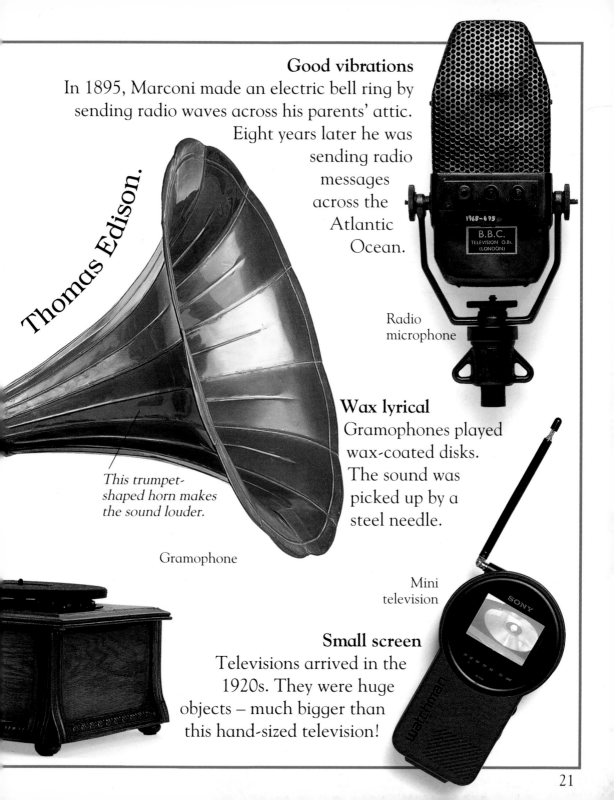

Good vibrations
In 1895, Marconi made an electric bell ring by sending radio waves across his parents' attic. Eight years later he was sending radio messages across the Atlantic Ocean.

Thomas Edison.

1968-695

B.B.C.
TELEVISION O.B.
(LONDON)

Radio microphone

This trumpet-shaped horn makes the sound louder.

Gramophone

Wax lyrical
Gramophones played wax-coated disks. The sound was picked up by a steel needle.

Mini television

SONY

watchman

Small screen
Televisions arrived in the 1920s. They were huge objects – much bigger than this hand-sized television!

Home help

Some inventions are very simple, but vital in our everyday lives. Imagine life without the toothbrush or the chair!

The first nylon toothbrush was Dr. West's "Miracle Tuft Toothbrush," manufactured in the US in 1938.

Toothbrush

From hidden codes to everyday chairs, your

A bar code consists of numbers and parallel lines.

Spectacles

Bar code

Check out
Bar codes carry information about a product. It is read by a laser and fed into a computer.

Eye to eye!
In 1280, Salvino Armati balanced two pieces of curved glass on either side of his nose to make the first pair of spectacles.

Wash and brush up
People cleaned their teeth with twigs or toothpicks until toothbrushes appeared in China in the 1400s.

home is full of ingenious inventions.

Seat of learning
The chairs that ancient Egyptians sat on 4,000 years ago were similar to this 19th-century chair with wooden arms and legs.

Regency-style dining chair

Originally tea bags were made of muslin.

In the bag
A paper tea bag holds the tea leaves in and allows water through its tiny holes. This way, you don't get tea leaves in the bottom of your cup!

Tea bag

23

G-BMNU

Take to the air!

For many hundreds of years all efforts to fly failed. Obviously birds knew something people didn't.

Hot-air balloon

Hot air
In 1783, the first people to fly were passengers in a hot-air balloon built by the Montgolfier brothers.

A rooster, a sheep, and a duck

Tail fin

Airfoil profile of wings gives plane lift.

Light aircraft

Winged wonders
Planes have come a long way since the Wright brothers made the first flight in 1903. But modern airplanes, like the Wrights' aircraft, are kept aloft because of the special airfoil shape of their wings.

Landing gear wheel

The first US shuttle, Columbia, was launched in 1981.

Space shuttle

Into space
Powered with enormous rocket engines, the space shuttle is the first reusable spacecraft. It flies into space on the back of a giant tank of fuel.

made the first flight – in a hot-air balloon.

Helicopter

Main rotor

G-BSUP

Tail rotor

A large rotor and small tail rotor keep the machine steady.

Round and round
In 1939, Igor Sikorsky came up with a basic design for the helicopter that is still used today.

Propeller

Aircraft are the fastest way to travel, as they can zip over mountains and seas.

25

Head for the water!

From the simplest reed or log rafts to the massive steel-clad ocean liners of today, boats have come a long way.

Chinese junk

Viking ship from AD 827

For business or pleasure, in war or

Sail away

Different types of sails have been used since the time of the ancient Egyptians. The Chinese favored a lugsail, or four-sided sail, for their junks.

Long haul

The Vikings built superb plank boats and sailed them across the Atlantic. These boats often had oars to give them extra speed.

Ship of the line

Huge ocean liners like the *Mauretania* were powered by steam turbines. More than 2,000 passengers can travel on a liner.

The *Mauretania*

peace, people will always sail the seas.

Down under

Built in 1624, the first submarine was made of wood and powered by 12 oarsmen. Today, some submarines are driven by nuclear power and carry missiles.

Nuclear submarine

Flying on air

Hovercrafts are faster than ships, because they "fly" above the water on a cushion of air.

Hovercraft

What's that?

Here are some mystery inventions. Most of them are early versions of devices that are familiar today. Can you guess what they do? The answers are on page 32.

3. Is this a coin meter?

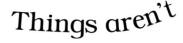

1. Is this a can opener?

Things aren't

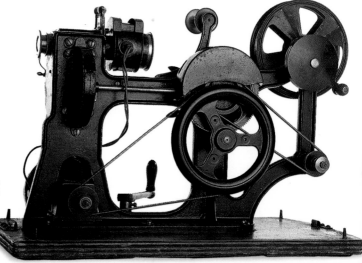

2. Is this a sewing machine?

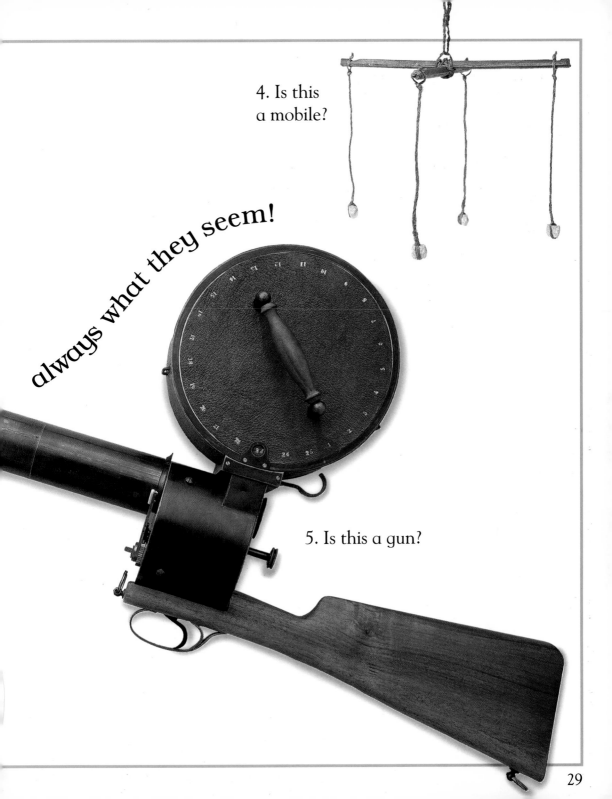

4. Is this
a mobile?

always what they seem!

5. Is this a gun?

Index

Five inventive questions

1. Did Edwin Land
invent
a. Land rovers
b. landscapes
c. the Polaroid camera?

2. In which year did
Thomas Edison invent
the phonograph?

3. Why is a Biro
called a Biro?

4. What powered the
first submarine?

5. Can you name the
passengers on the first
hot-air balloon trip?

Answers on page 32

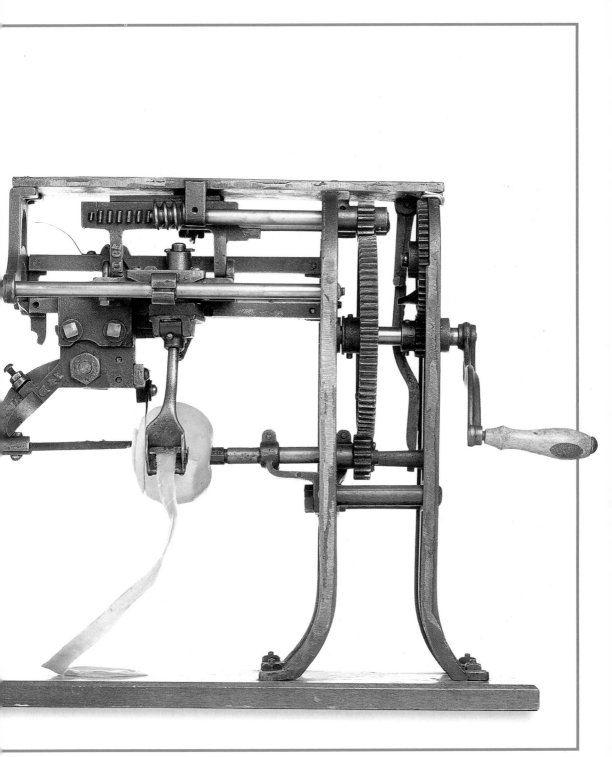

Answers

From page 28–29:
1. No, it's a Harrington Erado clockwork dental drill.
2. No, it's a home movie projector.
3. No, it's a midget camera.
4. No, it's an Egyptian groma, a surveyor's instrument.
5. No, it's a rifle camera!

From page 30:
1. The Polaroid camera
2. 1877
3. It is named after Georg and Josef Biro.
4. 12 oarsmen
5. A rooster, a sheep, and a duck